50 WAYS TO WEAR DENIM

Lauren Friedman

CHRONICLE BOOKS

SAN FRANCISCO

Library of Congress Cataloging-
in-Publication Data available.

ISBN 978-1-4521-4999-8

Manufactured in China

Design by Hillary Caudle

10 9 8 7 6 5 4 3 2 1

Chronicle Books LLC
680 Second Street
San Francisco, California 94107
www.chroniclebooks.com

To my father and brother,
who are as loyal and lovable as my favorite pair of jeans.

CONTENTS

INTRODUCTION

A Love Letter to Denim

There aren't many fabrics in our wardrobes that get better with age the way that denim does. In fact, there haven't been many items like denim that have so substantially filled the collective closet of human civilization. Denim is democratic; it cuts across social and class lines. But it's also egalitarian in a sartorial sense: Most pieces in your wardrobe would play quite nicely with a bit of denim. It's continuously fresh, yet amazingly unchanged since it first entered mainstream fashion; what looked good fifty years ago, by and large, still looks good today.

Denim stretches and softens much in the same way that we humans do over time. For some of us, our favorite pair of jeans is like the security blanket we clutched as babies—when we wear them, we know that all is right with the world. For others, denim is a talisman linking us to our past—and not just our individual past, but also our cultural past. Denim is durable and everlasting. Our connections to many of the denim items in our lives probably hold the record for the longest-running relationship any of us have ever had with a single article of clothing. (Many of us have known and loved our favorite pair of jeans longer than we've known our best friends!) Denim is by nature hardworking, yet how often do we really thank it for faithfully serving us every day that we reach for it in the closet or drawer?

This book, dear reader, is my love letter to denim. Denim and I—like you and your own denim—have enjoyed a lifelong relationship. There were the overalls I wore back throughout childhood—with knees that were always dirty from building forts in the backyard—that were as comforting as a hug from my mother. (To this day, I feel at once safe and adventurous when I wear overalls.) There were the boot-cut jeans I wore devotedly in high school until I slipped into my first pair of skinny jeans. (The thrill of that moment was as memorable as my first teenage crush.) And there are denim pieces I'm devoted to today—denim cut-offs, a pair of high-waisted flare jeans, an embroidered chambray shirt lifted from my dad's closet, to name just a few—that always make me feel like myself when I put them on.

Throughout the process of writing this book, I had the perfect excuse to invest in new denim pieces, like a new denim skirt, a denim jumpsuit, and a sparkling new pair of white jeans. But as I wrote and sketched, I also fell more deeply in love with the denim items I already owned, like my treasured jean jacket and a pair of untreated skinny jeans that I finally set out to break in. (And yes, I did jump into the ocean with them on, all in the name of research for the tips listed in look #10, "How to Break in Your Jeans.") This book is not intended to pressure you into buying new clothes (though I don't blame you if you are so inspired!), but rather to encourage you to recommit more fully to the ones you already own.

This book is also a head-to-toe fashion styling guide for wearing denim every day, for every occasion, and as a means for every form of self-expression you can imagine. Holding this book in your hands, you are heralding in a new era of denim adoration in your life. As you browse the looks and illustrations in these pages, picture your own cherished denim pieces. Picture too, the denim pieces and ensembles of your dreams—and make them a reality!

Let your creativity fly free.

—Lauren

THE SCHOOL OF DENIM

DENIM DICTIONARY

Get to know your denim! Here is a list of all the basic terms regarding your favorite fabric.

ABRASION: the process of making jeans look faded or worn by scraping, sanding, or rubbing the surface.

ACID WASH: a wash created not with acid but with pumice stones and bleach, patented by the Rifle Jeans Company in Italy in 1986.

BAR TACK: stitches that provide reinforcement in areas subject to wear and tear, such as pocket openings and zippers.

CHAMBRAY: a plain-woven, denim-like fabric with a crisscross weave (rather than the diagonal weave of denim fabric).

COTTON: the predominant fiber in denim fabric.

CROCKING: the process of dark denim dye rubbing off and bleeding onto skin or other fabrics.

GARMENT-DYED: a description of a garment that is dyed after it is made, rather than a garment that is made from dyed yarn.

HONEYCOMBS: faded lines seen at the back of the knees on a pair of jeans, named for their resemblance to a honeycomb pattern.

INDIGO DYE: a naturally occurring blue-colored compound found in plants traditionally used to color denim fabric.

LOOM: a device used to weave fabric.

RAW: a description of denim that has not been rinsed or prewashed.

RING-SPUN: a description of denim that is woven on older looms; characterized by tiny knots, or "slubs," that run through the yarn.

RIVET: a small metal tab used to reinforce pressure points in denim garments; first utilized by Levi Strauss & Co. in 1872.

SANFORIZE: a process that reduces denim shrinkage by stretching and manipulating raw denim before it is washed; developed in the 1920s and patented by Sanford Lockwood Cluett.

SELVEDGE: a slim woven band on the edge of denim fabric that prevents it from unraveling; derived from the term "self edge."

STONEWASH: a wash created by tumbling raw denim fabric with large stones that soften the denim, creating a worn-in appearance.

TWILL: a textile weave with a diagonal pattern, as seen in denim, which is one type of twill fabric.

WARP AND WEFT: the two yarns involved in the weaving process. The warp runs lengthwise and is dyed with indigo. The weft runs crosswise and is usually undyed.

WATCH POCKET: a small pocket often seen above the front pocket of a pair of jeans. Introduced by Levi's in 1902, it was originally intended for storing a pocket watch, but got progressively smaller as the use of pocket watches declined and is now referred to as a coin pocket.

WEAVE: to construct fabric by interlacing threads, often using a loom.

WEIGHT: a property of a fabric, measured in ounces, based on the density and heft of the yarn used to weave it.

WHISKERING: faded horizontal lines seen around the crotch and waist of jeans, named for their resemblance to a cat's whiskers.

YOKE: the V-shaped area located under the back waistline of a pair of jeans that helps create a curved seat.

white

bleached

light gray

gray

stonewash

seafoam

faded blue

true blue

light indigo

dark indigo

raw navy

black

GUIDE TO WASHES AND FINISHES

This illustration shows the most common denim washes and finishes. Originally, denim came in one hue—true blue!—that resulted from yarn being dyed with indigo before it was woven into denim cloth. Today synthetic dyes and a variety of washes and finishes are employed before and after weaving, resulting in a rainbow of hues.

TIPS FOR FINDING THE PERFECT PAIR OF JEANS

When picking out a new pair of jeans, consider that most denim fabric stretches out naturally over time. If you're between two sizes and you're going for a fitted look, select the smaller pair, as it will stretch to your natural curves with wear. And remember, the lighter and thinner the weight of the denim, the more it will stretch.

CARING FOR YOUR DENIM

Dirt is a good thing when it comes to denim—the less you wash it, the longer it will last! My jean jacket, which I've owned for more than fifteen years, has never touched a soap sud. It looks better than ever, and all it smells like is me. If you must wash your denim, first turn the garment inside out (to avoid fading), throw it in your washing machine, and select the cold-water setting. Hang to dry.

Beyond the washing machine? The sun is a wonderful natural disinfectant. To harness its cleaning powers, turn your denim inside out (unless you're going for a faded look) and hang it outside on a sunny afternoon. Others swear by putting their denim in a plastic bag and placing it in the freezer for up to a week, which can eliminate unwanted smells.

THE LOOKS

THE

PUSH OFF

HOW TO WEAR SKINNY JEANS

Skinny jeans are the figure-flaunting foundation on which any outfit can be built.

With skinny jeans down below, there's nothing you can't wear up top. Try . . .

slouchy tees haphazardly
tucked into the waist,

tunics, either belted for
definition or left relaxed,

men's-style button-
ups with the sleeves
pushed up,

oversize sweaters,

a long drapey scarf with
a statement overcoat,

or a bow-tied scarf
with a boxy blazer.

THE
Siren

HOW TO WEAR FLARE JEANS

This look has legs! Flare jeans are a traffic-stopping head-turner, thanks to the way they elongate your bottom half and flatter your backside. Liberate them from their hippie past with sleek, modern points and angles.

Pair flare jeans with . . .

a V-neck (the V shape adds additional length to the outfit),

a cropped blazer or jacket,

and boots that have a slightly pointed toe.

TIP: Pockets that are proportionately scaled to the size of your tush and sit slightly above the center of each cheek create a beautiful back view.

FUN FACT

The U.S. Navy adopted bell-bottoms into their uniform as early as the nineteenth century. The hems were easy to roll up, which was a convenient feature for sailors working barefoot on the decks.

THE
OFF-DUTY
STARLET

HOW TO WEAR BAGGY JEANS

Even on their days off, starlets
dress to impress—but they still
want to be comfortable. Cue
baggy jeans! They are sweetly
seductive when paired with
feminine tops and accessories—
and don't forget the lipstick!

Offset the relaxed fit of baggy jeans with . . .

a classic striped shirt and a dainty pair of flats,

a gingham button-up and plain canvas sneakers,

or a prim sweater and lovely high heels.

THE
PEG

HOW TO PEG YOUR JEANS

It's easy as 1-2-3! This quick trick can rein in the slack of a baggy pair of jeans or help spotlight a fabulous pair of shoes.

FUN FACT

Cowboys used the cuff of their jeans to hold a pack of cigarettes or as an ashtray when they roamed over dry flammable brush on the range.

For a great peg every time . . .

 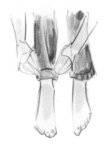 

1 Pull the front of the pant leg away from your body. Then fold it toward your opposite leg, creating a pleat.

2 Keeping a tight hold on the front of the pant leg, grab the bottom layer of denim and fold all fabric upward—once, then twice to secure the pleat. Adjust the tightness of the roll to your preference.

3 Repeat with the other pant leg.

Pair pegged jeans with traffic-stopping shoes, like . . .

lace-up ankle boots,

T-strap heels or pointy-toed pumps,

or flats, mules, or slides.

THE
Bon Vivant

HOW TO WEAR STRAIGHT-LEG JEANS

This debonair look says you enjoy the finer things in life: good food and drink, a thrilling performance, sublime literature, and—most important—an exquisite pair of jeans.

Get this look!

Start with immaculately
pressed straight jeans.

Add a crisp
button-up shirt

and a classic menswear-
inspired accessory, like
a tie or pocket square.

Top with a pinstriped
blazer, letting the cuffs
of your shirt peek just
so from the sleeves.

Slip into a handsome pair
of shoes, like brogues or
wing tips, freshly shined.

The finishing touch
is a pair of vintage
tortoiseshell sunglasses.

THE
Cornucopia

HOW TO WEAR COLORED JEANS

Colored jeans are a major food group in the denim diet. Wear them when you're hungry for a sartorial feast!

Colored jeans invite you to explore classic color combos, like . . .

red and blue,

pink and green,

or colors in the same family, like two shades of blue.

Colored jeans also make prints pop. Try pairing them with . . .

animal prints,

florals,

and stripes of all sizes.

7

THE

CAPTAIN

HOW TO WEAR WHITE JEANS

White jeans command attention
and brighten up any outfit. Wear
them when you want to shine!

How to wear white jeans year-round:

In cold weather, pair with cozy textures in muted shades, like navy and camel.	In summer, stay cool in white on white.	In any season, use white jeans as a blank canvas for showcasing your favorite colorful tops, shoes, and accessories.

8

THE

Midnight Poet

HOW TO WEAR BLACK JEANS

Black clothing doesn't have to be dark and moody. In *Funny Face*, a spunky Audrey Hepburn pirouettes and pliés through a jazz club wearing black head to toe. Channel her quirky spirit by pairing black jeans with black separates and accessories for a look that is confident yet feminine.

For a classic black-on-black look, pair black jeans with . . .

a black turtleneck   and a leather jacket.

Lighten the look with . . .

white tube socks,   black loafers (or   and a neat ponytail.
                             slip-on sneakers),

9

THE

Bold Italic

HOW TO WEAR STATEMENT JEANS

Statement jeans are
jeans that have been
embellished—for
example, distressed,
embroidered, or
made with patterned
denim—in a way that makes
them stand out in a crowd.
What do you want to say?
Say it with statement jeans!

Here are a few fashion statements you can make with embellished jeans:

Mix prints by combining patterned jeans with a top that features a different pattern.

Pair colorful, patch-covered jeans with a bright matching handbag.

Dress up distressed jeans with high heels and a blazer.

10

THE

Second Skin

HOW TO BREAK IN YOUR JEANS

When you're wearing the perfect pair of broken-in jeans, it can feel like you were born in them.

Start with a pair of dark-wash, untreated jeans, and break them in using one of these trusted methods.

1 Don't wash them for at least a few months.

2 Apply body oil after a shower and then put your jeans on as the oil sinks into your skin.

3 Wear them out for a night of sweaty fun on the dance floor.

4 For authentic sand-washed jeans, dive into the ocean and then roll around in the sand! Allow the jeans to dry on your body for thirty minutes (which helps them form to your curves), and then hang them to dry completely. If you'd like to freshen them up before wearing them, brush off the sand (it should come off easily once the jeans are dry), throw them in the washing machine, and hang to dry.

5 Can't make it to the beach to break in your jeans? Soak in a bathtub of lukewarm water for about ten minutes and then allow the jeans to dry on your body for at least thirty minutes. Then take them off and hang them until completely dry.

11

THE
WASP WAIST

HOW TO WEAR HIGH-WAISTED JEANS

Flaunt your waistline—and your hips, legs, and all the rest of you—with the ultimate figure-flattering cut. High-waisted jeans are gorgeous on every body type, and comfortable, too!

Not sure what to pair with those high-waisted jeans? Here's your go-to guide:

A deep V-neck shirt draws the eye down toward the high waist.

Long necklaces have a similar effect.

A crop top shows just a sliver of skin.

A tucked-in shirt shows off your waistline.

A belt adds definition to your middle.

If you want to add a layer, such as a jacket or a cardigan, make sure the bottom edge hits well below (or above) the hips.

12

THE

ANKLE-GRAZER

HOW TO WEAR CROPPED JEANS

Cropped jeans offer a seductive glimpse of your ankles. This look features flattering footwear, plus darling, face-framing accessories—because why should your ankles get to have all the fun?

The Ankle-Grazer features cropped jeans paired with . . .

a peplum top (characterized by a skirted bottom section), which helps define the waist and can make your legs appear longer,

a neckerchief or scarf (or a statement necklace) to add flair around the neckline,

lace-up espadrilles, which draw extra attention to the exposed ankles,

and a hat to top it all off.

Not just found on skinny jeans, a cropped leg suits all styles of jeans, including flared and baggy. Bonus points for eye-catching details at the hemline, like zippers or a frayed edge.

13

THE

Up and at 'Em

HOW TO WEAR ROLLED-UP JEANS

In this look, a no-nonsense roll of the hem is the finishing touch to an everyday, go-anywhere outfit.

Here are four ways to roll up your jeans, which work for every jean cut except flares.

The slight upturn: one small turn up of the hem, cute with flats.

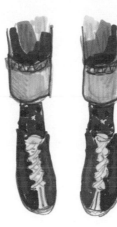

The big flip up: one large turn up of the hem, at least 2 in/5 cm tall, cool with bowling shoes and socks.

The narrow cuff: two neat folds up and over, about 1 in/2.5 cm wide, great for showing off ankle boots.

The wide cuff: two 1-in/2.5-cm rolls of the hem, works especially well with jeans that are wider.

TIP: If you find that you always roll your jeans the same way, consider sewing a few stitches into the roll to make it semi-permanent.

14

THE

WONDER WOMAN

- -

HOW TO WEAR JEANS WITH BOOTS

Boots and jeans are the ultimate
superhero duo. Pair your favorites
and stomp the streets in superfly
fashion.

TIP: For a leg-lengthening
look, wear jeans that are
a similar color to your boots.

Power up with one of these classic boots-jeans combos.

Straight-leg jeans
and cowboy boots

Baggy jeans and
chunky biker boots

Cropped jeans and
ankle boots

Boot-cut or flared jeans
and pointy-toe boots

Skinny jeans and
riding boots with socks
peeking out at the top

Skinny jeans and
over-the-knee boots

15

THE

TRUEST BLUE

HOW TO WEAR DENIM ON DENIM

In the world of denim, no two blues are exactly alike. This look celebrates the vast spectrum of blue hues by inviting you to wear multiple denim items at once.

Here are just a few ways to show off your Truest Blue:

Pair a denim vest
with a denim skirt.

Wear a chambray shirt
over a denim shirtdress,
and accessorize with a
belt around the waist.

Triple up your denim
in a pair of blue jeans,
a chambray shirt,
and a jean jacket.

16

THE
Baby Blues

HOW TO DRESS YOUR EYES IN DENIM

Denim isn't just a fabric—it's a state of mind. This simple make-up trick lets you incorporate your love for denim into your beauty routine.

For a denim-inspired smoky eye:

1 Using navy eyeliner, draw a thin line just above the lash line of your upper eyelid, starting at the inner corner of your eye. Make the line thicker as you extend it toward the outer corner of your lashes. Then line the thin, watery strip of your upper, inner eyelid from inner corner to outer corner.

2 Apply navy eyeshadow on your upper lid on top of the eyeliner and into the outer creases of your eyelids, brushing slightly upward in the outer corner to create a sideways V shape. To blend, use your brush to gently smudge the eyeliner and eyeshadow.

3 With a brush, dab a small dot of shimmery, light blue eyeshadow or blue glitter eyeliner on the middle of your eyelid, just above your lashes.

4 To finish the look, generously coat your eyelashes with navy mascara.

17

THE
ESSENCE

- -

HOW TO WEAR JEANS WITH
A WHITE T-SHIRT

This look, featuring a pair of jeans
and a simple white tee, distills
denim's legendary cool down to
its essence.

The Essence, three ways:

| Classic, pairing a crow neck tee with straight jeans and sneakers. | Sweet, pairing a scoop-neck tee with rolled-up jeans and flats. | Sultry, pairing a V-neck tee with flare jeans and sleek heels. |

To add polish . . .

Red lipstick is the ultimate accessory for this beautifully basic look.

18

THE
RABBLE-
ROUSER

HOW TO WEAR A JEAN JACKET

Incorporate a jean jacket into any outfit and watch it come to life—the jacket *and* the outfit. The instigator in your closet, the jean jacket goes with everything, and the options for layering are endless.

FUN FACT

Levi Strauss & Co. manufactured the original denim jacket as a "working blouse" in the late 1800s.

The jean jacket, worn six ways:

| With a boldly patterned scarf wrapped over the shoulders, | thrown over the shoulders, with the sleeves tied in front, | layered underneath another jacket, |

layered on top of a button-up shirt,

paired with a flirty dress,

or—classically cool— layered on top of a T-shirt, with the sleeves pushed up and collar popped.

19

THE
comrade

HOW TO WEAR A DENIM SHIRT

If clothes are companions, then the denim shirt is that loyal friend who always makes you feel your best. You can count on it to bring just the right amount of color, comfort, and style to any outfit.

A denim shirt can be worn . . .

slipped over a slim-cut, long-sleeved, patterned tee, and buttoned once below your ribs,

with the front shirttails tied together,

a few sizes too big, with a belt around the waist,

unbuttoned over a bathing suit at the beach,

buttoned all the way up to the top and layered under a crew-neck sweater,

or as a backdrop to a bow tied under the collar.

20

THE

RiNGLEADER

HOW TO CUFF THE SLEEVES
OF A DENIM SHIRT

A rolled-up sleeve says, "Let's get down to business." Cuff the sleeves of your denim shirt when you need your team to listen up and execute your brilliant ideas.

This sleeve-cuffing method ensures that the roll will stay secure:

Start with the sleeve
unbuttoned.

Fold up the sleeve
and pull the cuff
above your elbow.

Flip up the bottom of
the folded sleeve so it
covers all but the edge
of the cuff. Repeat on
the other sleeve.

21

THE

Curves Ahead

HOW TO MAKE A DENIM SHIRT
INTO A CROSS-BODY TOP

There's more than one way to tuck a shirt! Turn your denim shirt into a curve-hugging cross-body top with these simple steps.

This cross-body top is best paired with high-waisted jeans or a denim skirt that rises up to your belly button. To create this top:

1 Put on a denim shirt and leave it unbuttoned except for the button at the upper-middle of your torso.

2 Take the front flap of the shirt that has buttons and cross it over the other side of your body.

3 Tuck this flap into your pants or skirt as far to that side as it will go, making sure the tuck is tight and secure.

4 Repeat on the other side, wrapping the other flap across the front of your body in the opposite direction as far as it will go and tucking it in securely. To smooth any bulk, reach under your waistline and pull each flap toward your back.

22

THE

HEARTBREAKER

- -

HOW TO KNOT YOUR DENIM SHIRT

Knotting the shirttails of your denim shirt draws attention to your waist, creating a flirty, hourglass shape on any figure.

TIP: To raise the knot so it sits higher on your torso, just unbutton more buttons. To lower the knot, button more.

To knot your denim shirt . . .

1 Unbutton your denim shirt from the bottom up, stopping at the point on your torso where you want the knot to sit.

2 Bring both ends of the shirttail together and knot once, making sure that the shirttail without buttons is the one on top.

3 Flip the tails so they point in the opposite direction and then knot once more.

23

THE
Thunderbird

- -

HOW TO PERSONALIZE
YOUR DENIM

We've been personalizing our jeans for as long as we've been wearing them. By adding personal touches with a needle and thread, fabric scraps, or pins, you'll create a denim look that roars with originality.

Inspired by vintage fashion, here are some classic ways to personalize your denim:

Embroider your name on the thigh of a pair of jeans.

Patch the coat of your jeans with calico fabric.

Sew an old bandana on the inside hem so you see the fabric when you roll the cuffs of your jeans.

Pin a heart on the pocket of a chambray shirt.

Sew a secret pocket on the inside of a denim jacket.

Embroider your heart's desires across the back of a denim jacket.

24

THE
GAMINE

HOW TO WEAR DENIM
WITH STRIPES

Denim and stripes are a classic
duo. When worn with jeans, a
striped shirt calls to mind the
sun-bleached French Riviera
of the 1960s.

Show your true stripes by pairing . . .

a polished striped shirt, featuring stripes of any width,

with jeans (or shorts).

Add leather sandals, such as gladiators,

and a straw basket, with room for sunflowers!

THE
Star Pupil

HOW TO WEAR DENIM
WITH SEQUINS

Denim anchors sequined
clothing and accessories
for a high-low look that
can travel from day to night.
Shine on!

The Star Pupil, three ways:

Featuring your favorite pair of jeans and a sequined top.

Pairing a chambray shirt with a sequined skirt.

Layering a jean jacket over a sequined dress.

26

THE
MEOW MIX

- - - - - - - - - - - - - - - - - - - -

HOW TO MIX DENIM WITH
LEOPARD PRINT

Don't forget your
cat-eye sunglasses!
Denim worn with
leopard print is never
out of style.

There are endless ways to accessorize your favorite denim looks with leopard print. Add a spot or two . . .

on your feet,

as outerwear,

belted around your waist,

in your hand,

or draped around
your neck.

THE

COUNTRY CLUB ICONOCLAST

HOW TO WEAR DENIM WITH PLAID

Plaid can convey plenty of moods, but when paired with denim, it's a mix that's a hole in one.

Plaid and denim go hand in hand year-round.

In the fall, a coat in red and black plaid (known as buffalo plaid) is fetching when worn over denim on denim.

On a cozy winter afternoon, layer a plaid flannel shirt under (or over) a denim shirt.

In spring and summer, denim shortalls and a plaid scarf are a playful match.

28

THE

TIGRESS

HOW TO MIX DENIM WITH FAUX FUR

Like a big cat stalking the jungle, you'll command respect in this look that pairs denim with your faux-fur faves.

Get inspired by these furry pairings:

A faux-fur vest can be worn
over a jean jacket.

Skinny jeans offset a long faux-fur coat.

A faux-fur trapper hat goes
with a denim scarf,

while a faux-fur stole drapes regally
over the shoulders of a denim shirt.

29

THE
HI-FIDELITY

HOW TO WEAR A DENIM DRESS

A denim dress is comfortable and easy to move around in, and it shows off figures of every size and shape. Pair one with 1970s-inspired accessories for a confident, groovy vibe.

Denim dresses of every cut—be it a shirtdress, a shift dress, or an A-line shape—are flattered by these classic leather accessories. Try pairing your denim dress with . . .

a cross-body saddlebag,

a leather belt,

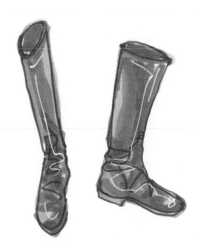

or riding boots with (or without) a heel.

30

THE

THROUGH the LOOKING-GLASS

HOW TO WEAR AN OVERSIZE DENIM SHIRT AS A SKIRT

In a world where up is down and shirts are skirts, this look fits right in. Featuring a denim shirt turned into a skirt, it boasts an eye-catching, tulip-shaped silhouette—and pockets, too!

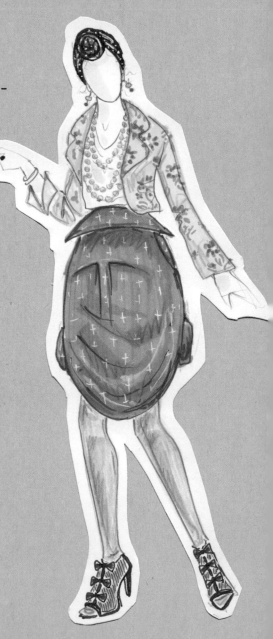

To temporarily turn your denim shirt into a skirt:

1 Unbutton an oversize denim shirt (if you don't have one, check the men's section of your favorite thrift store) and pull the sleeves inside out so they are hanging down through the inside of the shirt.

2 Wrap the shirt around your waist by placing the inside surface of the collar (the area that typically rests on the back of your neck) against the small of your back. Then bring each of the front shirttails around to the front of your torso. Begin buttoning up the shirt, starting with the bottom button and continuing up until the shirt sits snugly around your waist.

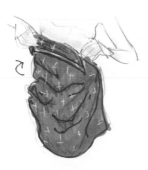

3 Rotate the shirt around so the buttons are now in the back.

4 Grab the sleeves that are hanging out from underneath the shirt. Bring each of them up and tuck them into the "pockets" created by the armholes.

31

THE
Lucky Strike

HOW TO WEAR A DENIM SKIRT

A denim skirt always scores a strike with any outfit. It can be dressed up or down, just like your favorite pair of jeans.

A denim skirt can be worn . . .

to the office, with knee-high boots, a tucked-in shirt, and a hip-length sweater,

on study dates, with a long untucked shirt layered under a schoolgirl sweater and paired with tights and clogs,

and while running errands, with a T-shirt, sandals, and a colorful, hold-everything bag.

FUN FACT

Denim skirts were not introduced into mainstream fashion production until the 1970s.

32

THE

Countess

- -

HOW TO TIE A DENIM SASH

Channel old-world femininity and
highlight your curves by donning
a sash-like denim bow around the
waist of a denim dress, jumper, or
oversize chambray shirt.

TIP: Don't have a denim
sash? Create one by
cutting the leg of an
old pair of jeans into a
long vertical strip that
can be hemmed or left
with a frayed edge.

Tying a denim sash is a lot like tying a bow—but upside down. Here's some guidance for the dexterously challenged:

1 Place the center of the denim sash against the small of your back and bring both ends forward, with the right side about 1 in/2.5 cm longer than the left.

2 Cross the right side over the left.

3 Knot once so the side that was originally on the right is now pointing upward, toward your head.

4 With your right hand, form a loop with the bottom tail and keep it clasped in your right hand.

5 With your left hand, take the top tail and cross it over and under the loop, creating a new loop. Pull the tail through the new loop to form the bow.

6 Straighten and adjust as needed.

33

THE

NEW FRONTIER

HOW TO WEAR DENIM OVERALLS

Not just for toddlers and railroad workers, a slim-cut pair of overalls worn with elevated extras proves to be a groundbreaking, modern look.

FUN FACT

The earliest written use of the term *overalls* was in 1776, when they were listed as part of the uniform for soldiers fighting in the American Revolution.

Glam up overalls with accessories like . . .

statement earrings,   a jeweled collar,   or lots of long, big necklaces.

The same goes down below. Glitzy footwear can offset the homespun vibe of overalls. Try . . .

a statement bootie,   a rolled-up cuff and sleek pumps,   or a gleaming pair of high-top sneakers.

34

THE

Prairie Wind

HOW TO WEAR A DENIM VEST WITH A DRESS

A denim vest calls to mind
a fresh-faced free spirit,
roaming the plains in
youthful rebellion. This
look pairs a vest with a
dress for prairie style
at its best.

These looks capture the many moods of the Prairie Wind.

Hunker down in a cardigan, worn underneath a denim vest.

Be one with the breeze in an unbuttoned blouse layered beneath a denim vest.

Battle the elements by wearing a vest under an army jacket . . .

or under a cape or shawl for a daintier option.

35

THE

PARTY CRASHER

- -

HOW TO WEAR DENIM SHORTS

A cute pair of jean shorts
will get you past any velvet
rope. Comfortable, sassy, and
unrestricting, they allow freedom
of movement, so you'll be ready
for anything.

The Party Crasher, three ways:

The Party Crasher Classic, featuring black tights, platform heels, a white shirt, a statement necklace, and a blazer.

The Party Crasher Dressy, featuring a statement top, a jeweled clutch, and nude-colored heels.

The Party Crasher Casual, featuring a blouse, a cashmere cardigan, and leather menswear-inspired shoes.

36

THE
Catch of the Summer

**HOW TO MAKE CUTOFF
DENIM SHORTS**

From the fishing hole to the beach to the hot city streets, nothing says summer like a pair of cutoffs.

To make cutoff denim shorts:

1 Start with a pair of oversize jeans. (Men's jeans work well.) Leaving at least a 3-in/7.5-cm inseam from the innermost point of the crotch, cut one leg at a slight angle, as shown above.

2 Fold the jeans lengthwise so the legs are neatly stacked on top of each other, with the cut leg on top. Cut the other leg carefully alongside the edge of the cut leg.

3 Unfold the jeans and make a ½-in/12-mm cut alongside the outer seam of each leg.

4 Cut off an additional portion of each front leg. Start by placing your scissor blades at the top of the outer seam cut and cutting downward at an angle, pointing the tips of your scissors toward the bottom of the inseam. NOTE: You will not cut length from the inseam; rather, you will cut in a way that produces a triangular scrap of fabric.

5 Repeat on the other side.

6 Put your cutoffs in the washing machine and dryer for a frayed-edge finish.

TIP: If you want to keep the pockets intact so they'll peek out from under the frayed edge, fold them up and pin them inside the waist of the jeans before you start cutting.

37

THE

Third-Wave Warrior

HOW TO WEAR A DENIM JUMPSUIT

For busy, empowered women who can't be bothered with elaborate outfits, the denim jumpsuit is the ultimate solution. Just hop in, zip it up, and you're off to pave the way of the future.

Here's how to get this look:

Layer a denim jumpsuit over a long-sleeve thermal tee.

Add kicky sneakers (or chunky wedges),

a fanny pack (or your favorite statement-making bag),

and finishing touches, like earthy, stylish silver jewelry

and oversize, vintage-inspired sunglasses.

38

THE
CUPID'S ARROW

HOW TO WEAR DENIM WITH JEWELRY

Leave them lovestruck by adding jewelry to your favorite denim looks. Providing a beautifully hued, not-too-dressy backdrop, denim is the perfect blank canvas for showcasing necklaces, bracelets, brooches, and more.

Fall in love with these denim-jewelry pairings:

Place a statement necklace under the collar of a denim shirt,

or unbutton your chambray shirt to reveal a tangle of necklaces lying against bare skin.

Lay a pendant on top of a collar buttoned all the way up,

or tuck a big chunky necklace under the collar of an open jean jacket.

Wear an oversize watch or bracelet over the cuff of a chambray shirt,

or pin a brooch or a collection of treasured pins on the chest area of a jean jacket or vest.

THE
LEFT BANK

HOW TO WEAR A SCARF WITH DENIM

A scarf around the neck embodies Left Bank chic. Pair a scarf with any denim garment and you'll achieve an irresistible *je ne sais quoi*.

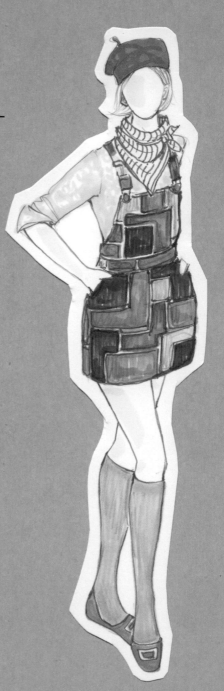

To try this versatile tie . . .

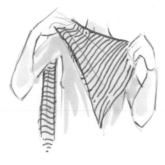

1 Drape a rectangular scarf that is 6 ft/1.8 m long over one shoulder so that most of it hangs down your back. Lift the inner corner of the front end of the scarf so the outer corner points down your chest. Hold the inner corner in your fingers for the duration of these instructions, using your other hand to complete the look.

2 Bring the other end of the scarf around the back of your neck and toward the front of your body, and then bring it underneath the front end.

3 Wrap it around your neck a second time, and this time bring it *over* the front flap.

4 Wrap it once more around your neck and then tie it to the corner of the other end that you've been holding in your fingers.

5 Tie the ends again for a double knot and then adjust as you see fit.

40

THE
SUGAR
PLUM

- -

HOW TO WEAR DENIM ON A DATE

This relaxed yet feminine look will comfortably take you from an afternoon coffee date to a romantic stroll in the park, or from dinner to the movies . . . and beyond.

TIP: Don't forget shoes that you can wear all night!

For a romantic look, try any of these variations:

The Sugarplum Sweet, featuring a jean jacket draped over the shoulders.

The Sugarplum Sour, featuring figure-hugging jeans and flirty flats.

The Sugarplum with a Twist, featuring a denim pencil skirt.

41

THE

BOSS

HOW TO WEAR DENIM TO WORK

The right kind of denim makes ideal office attire. Pair a smart blazer with dark-wash jeans, and the look can easily be taken from nine to five in many offices. Back to work!

To ace the denim review . . .

Carry a serious tote or briefcase in a dark color.

Stand tall in a sleek heel

Invest in a professional blouse that has personality.

Know your denim. Dark wash is best for many workplaces, and the most suitable cuts are straight, skinny, and flare (particularly flares with a wide hem).

Wearing a navy pinstriped suit with a chambray shirt is another way to wear denim to work.

42

THE

NEW SCHOOL

- -

HOW TO WEAR DENIM WITH ATHLETIC GEAR

Denim adds a graceful edge to athletic-themed outfits, taking sporty gear out of the gym and stadium and into your everyday wardrobe.

Root for your team in style with one of these winning combinations.

Pair a denim skirt with a football or hockey jersey.

Top a look from the gym—spandex, basketball shorts, boxing gloves—with a jean jacket.

Upturn the collar of a denim vest and wear with a baseball cap.

Wear cropped jeans to show off sporty kicks.

43

THE

MODERN REDUX

- -

HOW TO WEAR DENIM
TO A DRESSY EVENT

Denim wants to be taken
someplace fancy, too!
Dressing it up with
exceptionally refined
pieces is for the brave
guest who isn't afraid to
toe the line of convention.

Dress denim to the nines by donning . . .

a very fine chambray
shirt under a tuxedo,

a pair of jeans with a
winged-collar tuxedo shirt,
bow tie, cummerbund,
and ornate jewelry,

a jean jacket, worn off
the shoulders with an
extravagant ball gown,

a jean jacket over
a camisole and a
floor-length skirt,

or, as the ultimate
"something blue,"
wear a jean jacket with
a wedding dress.

Ultra-special accessories
are a must, like a frothy,
decadent pair of
high heels, or a gem-
encrusted clutch.

44

THE
Penny Edition
HOW TO WEAR DENIM WHEN RUNNING ERRANDS

Running errands doesn't have to be all business. Dress for the occasion by pairing jeans with a favorite scarf, jacket, and loafers. It's the perfect look for dashing out for groceries or swinging by the bank or newsstand. Don't forget your reusable tote!

Broken-in, well-loved jeans are chic and comfortable—perfect for getting stuff done. Pair with these hot-off-the-press picks:

| A sporty anorak and a silk scarf. | A wool blazer and an eye-catching wrap. | A bomber jacket with a plaid muffler. |

TIP: Put a shiny penny in your loafers for good luck!

45

THE

Point-and-Shoot

HOW TO WEAR DENIM WHEN GETTING YOUR PHOTOGRAPH TAKEN

Ever wondered what to wear for that passport photo, headshot, or profile pic? For a look that conveys effortless poise, pair slim-cut jeans with a crisp denim shirt and accessorize with jewelry that complements your eyes.

Eyes of every color will shine against a denim-on-denim outfit, especially with these enhancements:

An emerald ring if you have green eyes.

A lavender necklace if you have hazel eyes.

An amber brooch if you have brown eyes.

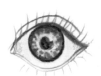

TIP: Make every angle your best with a rosy pink lipstick color a few shades darker than the natural tone of your lips. It will add a natural glow to your face without screaming "I'm wearing lipstick!"

Icy blue earrings if you have blue eyes.

46

THE
ELEMENTS

HOW TO WEAR DENIM
IN HARSH WEATHER

You can dress for warmth and protection and be chic at the same time. Denim serves as a breathable extra layer for every kind of passing storm.

Whatever the weather, denim's got you covered.

When dressing for warmth, wear a denim dress over skinny jeans and a turtleneck.

For shoveling snow, layer baggy jeans over long johns and add a parka and sturdy boots.

When there's a chance of rain, wear a denim vest under a trench coat for a prepared, ready-for-anything look.

TIP: Start a collection of cold-weather accessories that make you happy every time you have to put them on, like cashmere-lined gloves or a hand-knitted scarf.

47

THE
HOBBYIST

HOW TO WEAR HEAVY-DUTY DENIM

Originally designed for laborers in the American west, denim can withstand more than a little bit of wear and tear. Don some denim when getting down and dirty with your favorite chores and pastimes.

What do you like to do? Do it in denim!

Wear a denim apron while baking and gardening,

a jumpsuit for painting projects,

relaxed jeans for cleaning marathons,

high-waisted jeans with fishing waders,

and skinny jeans for horseback riding.

48

THE

FLIGHT SCHOOL

HOW TO WEAR DENIM WHEN TRAVELING

Hoping for an upgrade to the first class cabin? Ditch the sweats and spandex and don your best pair of jeans. This look ensures that you'll be presentable when you travel—and comfortable, too!

Embark on your next adventure wearing a polished pair of jeans and . . .

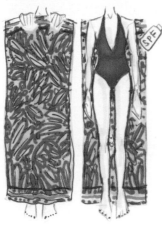  

a wrap that can double as a scarf or a blanket,	slip-on shoes,	and an exotic find from your past travels, such as a carpet bag or beaded jewelry.

TIP: A denim skirt is a wrinkle-free option when you have to look presentable for business travel or a dressy restaurant reservation.

49

THE
Weekender

HOW TO WEAR DENIM WITH LOUNGEWEAR

Dying for a morning coffee but not ready to take off your cozy pajamas? Need an excuse to wear that favorite, beat-up sweatshirt all weekend long? Just add denim! Denim brings a structured element to your most relaxed weekend pieces, so you can get out and about without leaving the comforts of home.

For a chic and cozy fashion statement, wear:

a slim cropped jean with
a silk pajama shirt,

a jean jacket with sweatpants
or pajama bottoms,

a denim vest over a
zip-up sweatshirt,

or a chambray shirt under
a sweatshirt.

THE
NEVER-ENDING STORY

- - - - - - - - - - - - - - - - - -

HOW TO RECYCLE
YOUR DENIM

Denim is an inherently "green" fabric. It never goes out of style, it only looks better with age and wear, and it is so durable that it can be transformed into an entirely different, like-new item of clothing. This look is inspired by a skirt my mom made out of an old pair of Lee jeans, to which she added fabric scraps and trinkets she found on the shores of Lake Michigan.

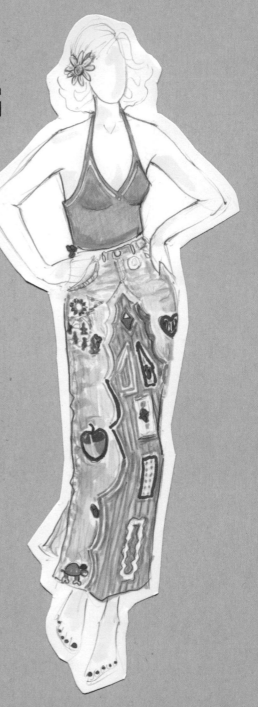

Reduce and reuse by . . .

turning your jeans into a skirt and sewing on items that tell your personal story,

sewing up the leg of a pair of jeans to create a purse or pouch,

cutting off the legs of a pair of overalls or the sleeves of a jean jacket, and saving the scraps for future sewing projects,

such as lining a box with strips of cut-up denim to create a denim-lined jewelry box.

Or donate your denim to a denim recycling program and help turn it into currency!

THE HISTORY OF DENIM

1492:
Christopher Columbus outfits his ship with sails made from the most durable fabric available, a rough, early form of denim.

1600S:
Members of the Italian navy wear trousers made out of denim manufactured in Genoa, Italy. One theory about the origin of the term *jeans* is that it comes from Genes, the French name for the town of Genoa.

1848:
James W. Marshall discovers gold in Coloma, California, prompting a wave of expansion as people rush westward toward the possibility of getting rich quickly. Durable denim is the fabric of choice for gold panners, miners, and railroad workers involved in developing the west.

1872:
Pioneering tailor Jacob Davis is inundated with complaints that the seams of the denim pants he is selling to workers aren't tough enough to withstand the stresses of hard labor. To address these complaints, he reinforces the seams with rivets originally used for horse blankets. Davis then teams up with Bavarian immigrant Levi Strauss, a wholesale goods supplier based in San Francisco, to patent and manufacture their new ultra-sturdy pants.

1873:
Levi Strauss & Co. opens its first blue jeans factory in San Francisco.

1866:
Philip Danforth Armor opens the first meatpacking plant in Chicago, ushering in an increased demand for beef. Ranchers and cowboys, usually outfitted in head-to-toe denim, spread across

the open range, from Texas to California, the Rocky Mountains and Nevada, with increasing numbers of cattle.

1939:
John Wayne mythologizes the iconic figure of the cowboy in his breakout role in *Stagecoach*. Wayne wears dusty, worn-in blue jeans, suspenders, neckerchief, and cowboy hat in the film, and he will continue to wear denim throughout his western movie career.

1943:
A young Lauren Bacall is photographed for the cover of *Harper's* *Bazaar* in a denim popover dress designed by Claire McCardell, the first American designer to reimagine denim for women.

1944:
The world gasps when women of Wellesley College are captured wearing jeans in a photograph featured in *Life* magazine in 1944, dubbed "the sloppy look." In response, the students write a letter to *Life*, stating "We do not sympathize with stringy hair and baggy shirts, but we will fight to the death for our right to wear dungarees on the proper occasions."

1945: Returning home from Japan at the end of World War II, American soldiers leave behind much of the denim they wore while on leave, igniting an international demand for jeans and sparking Japan's love for authentic, old-school-style denim that continues to this day.

1948:
Hollywood actor Robert Mitchum is arrested for the possession of marijuana and serves a sixty-day sentence in the county jail. While he is serving time, iconic images of him in a head-to-toe denim

prison uniform are released to the public.

1951:
Levi Strauss & Co. makes a denim tuxedo for crooner Bing Crosby after he was notoriously turned away from a Vancouver hotel for wearing jeans. The label inside the denim tuxedo includes instructions that the wearer should be "duly received and registered with cordial hospitality."

1952:
Actress Eartha Kitt appears in the pages of *Life* magazine playing a game of pickup baseball with some neighborhood boys in Central Park while wearing denim shorts, a white shirt, and a head scarf.

1953:
Marlon Brando overturns some of the homespun, wholesome feel traditionally associated with denim by wearing his with a leather jacket and a defiant, sultry swagger in *The Wild Ones*.

1955:
Rebel Without a Cause, starring James Dean, is released. Denim's place as a uniform of the counterculture is solidified on the silver screen when Dean sports jeans and a tight white T-shirt, playing a role that represents defiance against the primness of the previous generation.

1961:
Marilyn Monroe proves that women can also wear denim with rebellious sex appeal while wearing jeans and a jean jacket in the movie *The Misfits*.

1969:
Although denim originally marked the wearer as an outlier, by the 1960s the fabric was de rigueur for almost every flower child of the counterculture movement, epitomized by the Woodstock

Festival that occurred during this year.

1970–71:
Denim is the cover star of two hit albums—Neil Young's *After the Gold Rush* (1970), which features Young's behind in a pair of patched-up jeans, and Elton John's *Madman Across the Water* (1971), which depicts the album's song list embroidered on a scrap of denim. More than a decade later, denim makes an iconic appearance on the front cover of Bruce Springsteen's *Born in the U.S.A.* (1984).

1970S:
Jeans take a rougher, louder turn in this decade when the fabric is embraced by the punk movement. Rockers such as the Ramones, Patti Smith, and Debbie Harry sport shredded denim with leather jackets, faded T-shirts, and a smirk.

1970:
Fashion designer Yves Saint Laurent, who famously declared, "I have often said that I wish I had invented blue jeans . . . They have expression, modesty, sex appeal, simplicity—all I hope for in my clothes," sends denim on its first trip down the runway in his fall/winter 1970 collection.

1976:
Inspired by European jean brands, Gloria Vanderbilt creates the first line of "designer" jeans for her namesake label.

1978:
Calvin Klein bursts onto the jean scene with pro-vocative ads, first starring Patti Hansen and then Brooke Shields, who in 1980 famously purred, "Nothing comes between me and my Calvins."

1984:
Levi Strauss & Co. is the outfitter of the Summer Olympics U.S. team.

1988:
Anna Wintour, for her groundbreaking first cover at American *Vogue* in 1988, dresses model Michaela Bercu in a Christian Lacroix jacket and jeans.

1991:
Kurt Cobain, the lead singer of Nirvana, ushers in an era of '90s grunge while sporting flannel shirts and tattered jeans.

1992:
Partially responsible for the 1990s-era trend of baggy, oversize jeans that sag to the knees, brands FUBU and Phat Farm are founded this year. Embraced by the hip-hop community, these labels will help inspire rappers such as Jay Z (cofounder of Rocawear) and Sean "Puff Daddy" Combs (founder of Sean John) to start their own clothing lines, which include baggy jeans in their offerings.

1996:
British fashion designer Alexander McQueen introduces "bumster" pants—which were so low-cut in the back that they exposed the upper tush—igniting a craze for low-rise jeans.

2000:
Rock-chic fashion icon Kate Moss revives the skinny jean.

2001:
Britney Spears and Justin Timberlake appear at the MTV Video Music Awards in matching denim ensembles, ushering in an era of denim-friendly red-carpet looks.

2003:
Saturday Night Live debuts "Mom Jeans," a parody commercial advertising an unflattering style of jeans for moms.

2010:
Jeggings—skin-tight leggings that resemble a pair of jeans—are reported to be one of the most popular clothing trends of the year.

2011:
Barbie releases Barbie Basics, a line of collector's-edition dolls wearing wardrobe basics like T-shirts, little black dresses, and, of course, jeans.

2016:
Hotter than ever, denim is featured in the runway collections of luxury brands, including Chanel and Louis Vuitton, while Levi's—whose denim business is now nearly 150 years old—reigns as the "it" denim brand.

SUGGESTIONS FOR FURTHER READING

The following books provided information and inspiration during the creation of this book. You might enjoy them too!

Current, Emily, Meritt Elliott, and Hilary Walsh. *A Denim Story: Inspirations from Bellbottoms to Boyfriends*. New York: Rizzoli International Publications, 2014.

Harris, Michael Allen. *Jeans of the Old West: A History*. Atglen, PA: Schiffer Publishing Ltd., 2010.

Mettler, Lizzie Garrett. *Tomboy Style: Beyond the Boundaries of Fashion*. New York: Rizzoli International Publications, 2012.

Sullivan, James. *Jeans: A Cultural History of an American Icon*. New York: Gotham Books, 2006.

Thomas, Isabelle and Frédérique Veysset. *Paris Street Style: A Guide to Effortless Chic*. New York: Abrams Image Edition, 2012.

Tuite, Rebecca C. *Seven Sisters Style*. New York: Rizzoli International Publications, 2014.

ACKNOWLEDGMENTS

I would like to thank the many people who helped make this book possible: Elizabeth Yarborough, Hillary Caudle, Jennifer Tolo Pierce, and the entire Chronicle Books staff for their support in bringing these denim dreams to life. The online Wellesley community, the Denver Art Museum, and Florence Müller for research help in a pinch. My dear friends and anyone with whom I ever talked about denim in the past two years (you know who you are); those conversations about the diverse relationships we have with our denim were truly the sparks that ignited this book. My mom, dad, and brother for everything. My uncles, aunts, and cousins for cheering the loudest. And lastly, my grandmother Enid who passed away before the completion of this book. I tacked a photograph of her onto my denim inspiration board and referred to it many times during the writing process. In it, she is smiling and wearing high-waisted jeans and a cream cable-knit sweater—an elegant, relaxed outfit that reveals her luminous, best self. She became my ultimate denim muse. My hope is that this book will inspire you, dear reader, to style your own denim in ways that bring out your most beautiful and most fulfilled self.